W9-AUO-202

To
My Husband
with
Love

To My Husband *with* Love

Allen Appel

ST. MARTIN'S PRESS NEW YORK

www.stmartins.com

Book design by Judith Stagnitto Abbate

ISBN 0-312-28667-8

First Edition: February 2002

10 9 8 7 6 5 4 3 2 1

To
My Husband
with
Love

Thanks, Dear,

for...

Thanks, Dear, for...

Noticing me.

Asking me out.

Asking me out again.

*C*hoosing me over all the other
girls you could have had.

*W*anting to be with me.

*W*anting to stay with me.

Luring me with your siren song.

Thanks, Dear, for...

Pursuing me.

Thanks, Dear, for...

Persevering, even though my
father was against it.

*B*eing handy.

Thanks, Dear, for...

———◆———

*B*eing willing to try many home
repairs, even though things don't
always work out. I'll love you
anyway, even if you have to call
in a professional.

*L*ifting.

*H*auling.

*C*arrying.

Thanks, Dear, for...

Moving furniture. And then
moving it again.

And again.

All without complaint. Or without
too much complaint.

Thanks, Dear, for...

*B*eing the Grillmaster.

Cooking. Every once in a while. Even though it's not one of your natural skills.

Thanks, Dear, for...

*H*elping out.

*T*aking out the garbage.

*P*ainting.

Mowing the lawn.

Thanks, Dear, for...

Carving.

MEATS

Giving me a bite.

*K*nowing when you've had enough.

*Q*uitting smoking.

*A*t least trying to quit smoking.

Thanks, Dear, for...

Asking for my opinion.

Asking for my help.

Not being ashamed to ask for help
even when you know you're going
to look stupid.

Thanks, Dear, for...

---

*T*aking me seriously.

*R*especting my:

Ideas

Work

*R*especting me.

Thanks, Dear, for...

Listening intently. Or at least looking like you are.

Listening to me drone on about my problems at work even if you don't know the people or care what I'm talking about.

Thanks, Dear, for...

*T*aking my suggestions, even when
you don't think it's such a great idea.

Not holding a grudge, even when
I've really screwed up.

Thanks, Dear, for...

Looking on the bright side.

*E*xplaining things, when they need
to be explained, without acting like
a know-it-all.

Thanks, Dear, for...

Explaining about:
Cars.
Sports.
What men really want.

Even if I already knew most of it.
Especially the part about what men
really want.

*K*eeping track of our financial
affairs. Such as they are.

Not criticizing my driving, even
though I know it's killing you.

Not lording it over me when
I get a ticket.

———◗◆◖———

*K*nowing when to keep your
mouth shut in general.

Thanks, Dear, for...

*R*emembering our anniversary.
Even if you need a little help.

*T*aking me on some excellent
vacations.

*P*utting gas in my car, and
checking the oil and the tires.
I'm really going to try to do better
with this. I know it's important,
God knows you've told me
enough times.

*U*nderstanding that we were created as equals and treating me as such. Most of the time. Except when it concerns sports or car maintenance.

*K*nowing I can take care of myself.

Thanks, Dear, for...

*L*oving me.

*B*eing kind.

*A*musing me.

Making me laugh.

Laughing with me.

Not laughing at me.

Thanks, Dear, for...

Showing a girl a good time.

*B*eing my knight in shining armor.
Even if the armor needs polishing
every once in a while.

Sharing.

Never letting me down.

Not being a show-off. Usually.

Showing affection, even in public.

Thanks, Dear, for...

*F*orgiving me.

Thanks, Dear, for...

*F*orgiving me again. I know it's hard sometimes. But I swear I'm going to pay more attention to my car maintenance.

*F*ighting fair (pretty fair).

*K*nowing when to give in.

*K*nowing when to let me win.

Thanks, Dear, for...

Not holding it against me when I
seem to be overreacting a bit.

Being reasonable when you're
angry. (Well, wouldn't it be nicer if
you were?)

Taking constructive criticism
pretty well. Under the
circumstances. Most of the time.
Some of the time.

Thanks, Dear, for...

*M*aking up after a fight.

*B*eing a big enough man to admit
it when you know I'm right and
you're wrong.

Worrying.

Keeping fit. I know you're going
to start any day now.

Thanks, Dear, for...

*H*umoring me. I know some of the
things I ask you to do seem sort of
silly, but . . .

Thanks, Dear, for...

*B*eing a gentleman.

*B*eing a good provider.

Thanks, Dear, for...

Going for walks, even when you
have other things on your mind.

*G*oing shopping with me.

*G*oing to events you hate just to humor me and not acting like a pill about it.

Thanks, Dear, for...

*B*eing cool.

*B*eing exceptionally cool.

*B*eing honest.

*B*eing my friend.

*B*ringing me flowers.

Thanks, Dear, for...

—————◦⊱✦⊰◦—————

Dancing.

Dancing, even though you
don't like to.

————◆►◄◆————

*D*ancing with my mother at the
wedding.

*G*etting along with my parents
(not the easiest thing in the world).

*N*ot treating me the way your
father treats your mother.

Thanks, Dear, for...

---

*B*uying me presents yourself and
not just saying, "Go pick out
something you like."

Thanks, Dear, for...

*B*ringing drama into my life.

Being patient, even when I'm
being overly dramatic.

*N*ot seeing our marriage the way
some of your friends see theirs.

*B*ragging about my finer points.

*T*aking care of me.

*T*aking care of yourself.

*D*ressing up without complaint
when the occasion demands it.

Thanks, Dear, for...

*K*eeping tidy.

Not mentioning my wrinkles.

Thanks, Dear, for...

Not minding that I've put on a
few extra pounds.

In fact, not mentioning any of my imperfections.

*K*nowing when to turn a blind eye
in general. It's a useful skill many
men never learn.

Not snoring. Ha ha.

I know you can't help it.

Thanks, Dear, for...

*U*nderstanding that I have nothing to wear and need to buy some new clothes. Even though it looks like my closet is pretty full.

Thanks, Dear, for...

Letting me have the bigger closet.

Understanding that just because it appears that I have enough shoes, I don't really.

Thanks, Dear, for...

---

*J*ust being a swell guy.
Most of the time.

*B*eing so suave.

*B*eing so manly.

*B*eing such a take-charge guy.

Thanks, Dear, for...

*T*urning up the thermostat even
though you don't think it's cold
in the house.

*G*etting out of bed and turning off
the television.

Thanks, Dear, for...

*C*hecking for burglars in the
middle of the night even though it's
cold out of the bed and there's never
really been a burglar downstairs but
I distinctly heard something and it
doesn't hurt to be careful.

*G*etting up to turn off the light,
check the stove, and make sure the
doors are locked. Like I said, it
doesn't hurt to be careful.

*B*eing gentle.

*B*eing rough, gently.

Thanks, Dear, for...

*R*omance.

*B*ack rubs.

*F*ront rubs.

*B*eing flexible and open-minded
when I come up with something
new I'd like to try.

Thanks, Dear, for...

*M*aking love.

*B*eing sweet.

*T*rying to keep up when I'm
feeling especially frisky.

*T*hose great massages.

*H*aving poetry in your soul, if not exactly on your lips.

Thanks, Dear, for...

*H*olding hands.

Not making a fool of yourself
around other women.

------➤●◄------

Surprising me with your unbridled
passion. (I think I'm going to faint!)

*T*hinking that I'm beautiful.

*K*eeping me satisfied.

Thanks, Dear, for...

*E*volving, over the years, into a
damn fine husband.

*T*elling me you love me. Even if you need a little prompting.

*B*eing faithful. Always and forever.

*U*s. Always and forever.